The Vale of Rheidol Railway

Rheilffordd Cwm Rheidol

A Visitors Guide, containing a brief history of the railway, recent achievements and details of locomotives and rolling stock, together with what can be seen on a journey along the beautiful valley of the Afon Rheidol.

Compiled and Edited By

Allan C Baker.

ISBN: 0-9544546-0-X

Published by: The Phyllis Rampton Narrow Gauge Railway Trust,
Highfield House,
High Halden,
Kent. TN26 3LD.

Distributed By: The Vale of Rheidol Railway,
Park Avenue, Aberystwyth,
Ceredigion. SY23 1PG
(registered Charity No 1076037)
Telephone: Aberystwyth (01970) 625819
Fax: Aberystwyth (01970) 623769
www.rheidolrailway.co.uk

Designed, Produced and Printed by:
Aquarius Press Ltd
Ashford, Kent
Telephone: 01233 662544

Cover picture
Locomotive No 8 and train having just left Nantyronen on 29 August 2001,
and heading for Devil's Bridge. (photograph by LG Marshall)

Early coloured postcard photograph of a train heading up the valley approaching Quarry Cutting, and almost at the end of the climb to Devil's Bridge. The locomotive is No 2 PRINCE of WALES. This card was published by the Pictorial Stationary Co, of London and posted in Birmingham on 19 November 1908, with a halfpenny (old - almost immeasurable in present currency!) stamp.

Another old postcard view of a train approaching Devil's Bridge and just before Quarry Cutting. This card was published by Raphael Tuck & Sons, was posted in Aberystwyth on 2 July 1906, with a holiday greeting to a friend in Shrewsbury.

One more old picture postcard view, this time of Devil's Bridge station showing a well loaded train having just arrived. This is a scene readily recognisable today - see page 22. The card was published by Photochrom of London and Tunbridge Wells, but in this case has never been posted.

A further old postcard view of an up train having just passed Rhiwfron, and on the Nant-ar-fynwg (meaning the stream on the precipice) curve, with the Derwen forest to the right. Notice the Afon Rheidol in the valley below, and the route of the railway curving round the hillside in the upper background. In the distance across the valley can just be discerned the Cwm Rheidol Mine. This is a card published locally by HH Davies of Aberystwyth, posted in the town on 27 September 1913, with a holiday message to Southport.

VALE OF RHEIDOL LIGHT RAIL-WAY. [H.L.]

AN

ACT

(As Amended in Committee)

For making a Light Railway between Aberystwyth and Devil's Bridge in the County of Cardigan and for other purposes.

60 & 61 VICT.—SESSION 1897.

ARTHUR J. HUGHES,
Aberystwyth,
Solicitor for the Bill.

W. & W. M. BELL,
27, *Great George Street, Westminster,*
Parliamentary Agents.

Geo. Kelly & Co., 11 & 13, King-street, Westminster, S.W., Printers.
(s)

A page from the original Act
Parliament for the construction of t
railway dated 6th August 18.

Foreword

The Vale of Rheidol Railway was purchased from The British Railways Board in 1989 by the Brecon Mountain Railway, under the provisions of the Transport Acts 1968 and 1981. The Brecon Mountain Railway is a narrow gauge tourist railway and at the time was owned by AJ (Tony) Hills and Peter J Rampton, and these two gentlemen therefore, were in effect the purchasers from The British Railways Board of the VoR. Subsequently, Peter Rampton exchanged his interest in the Brecon Mountain Railway for Tony Hills interest in the VoR.

The Vale of Rheidol Railway is now supported by The Phyllis Rampton Narrow Gauge Railway Trust (PRNGRT), a registered charity No 292240, formed on 10 July 1985. The PRNGRT has as its objectives: Shall be to preserve, exhibit, display and to loan for demonstration for the public benefit and for the advancement of technical, historical and general education, steam and other railway locomotives, rolling stock, equipment, machines and relics which are (a), of historical, operational and general interest and in addition (b), of educational value. To this end, as well as supporting the Vale of Rheidol Railway the Trust has purchased for the Railway a sizable collection of largely but not exclusively, British built locomotives and rolling stock from all over the World, for eventual display, and occasional use on the Vale of Rheidol Railway. There are plans to build a Museum at Aberystwyth to display some of these exhibits, as well a large collection of other narrow gauge railway memorabilia that has been assembled, including an archive of material relating to narrow gauge railways, and the locomotive and rolling stock building industry World wide. These plans are extremely long term, have been under development for several years, but it is hoped that significant progress can be made over the next few years in bringing at least some of them to fruition. A number of the locomotives that have been acquired can be seen on the railway, and others are in store in various parts of the country, including one that has been restored to as near as possible 'as built' working condition.

It is hoped that this small booklet, primarily intended as a guide to visitors of the railway, will nonetheless, go some way to ensuring that the Trust's objectives are known. It has also been a number of years since a guide book of the Vale of Rheidol Railway has been available for visitors, to tell not only what it strives to achieve, but also a little of its history. It is also the Trust's intention, henceforth, to regularly issue updated versions of this slim volume to illustrate not only progress on the Vale of Rheidol Railway itself, but also the Trust's other objectives, and restoration to display condition of its assets.

In compiling this slim volume, which has given me great pleasure, I have of course, been assisted by my fellow Trustees, along with the Manager of the Railway, Neil Thompson. Neil and his small team are largely responsible for the splendid turn out of locomotive and train you travel in, as well as the excellent condition of the permanent way. If visitors and anybody else interested in the Railway, feel that other ancillary issues have been somewhat neglected, it has been in the quest to ensure the long term future of the locomotives, rolling stock, track formation and permanent way, on which extremely large sums of money have had to be expended. To renew the entire 12 miles of track and sleepers, renew the bridge at Llanbadarn as well as other formation improvements, and put the locomotives and rolling stock into the condition you see them now, has taken a long time, a lot of resources, and a large sum of money!

Other helpers have included Roger Hateley who has also been of great help with his cartography skills, and I cannot thank him enough, along with fellow Trustee TD Allen Civil. I have also consulted the library of The Narrow Gauge Railway Society. The photographs or either from the Trust's collection, of my taking or are credited individually, and special thanks are due to those who have allowed their use. Any readers wanting to find out more about this fascinating little railway, perhaps the finest, and certainly the least spoilt of all those surviving in North Wales, if not the entire country, are referred to the books listed in the short Bibliography at the rear of this book. All the volumes listed are well worth a study.

Allan C Baker   February 2003.
Trustee,
Phyllis Rampton Narrow Gauge
Railway Trust,
c/o Vale of Rheidol Railway, Aberystwyth.

The Train Service

The train service, whilst varying slightly from year to year, generally consists of two trains in each direction per day for much of the season, increasing to four in late July and August, as well as at Bank Holiday periods, but only on Mondays to Thursdays. When two trains are running one will leave Aberystwyth at mid morning and the other early afternoon, the journey taking approximately one hour, and the train remaining at Devil's Bridge for about the same time. Obviously, if passengers want to spend more time at Devil's Bridge, and it is recommended they should, and they have travelled on the early train, they can return on the later one. When four trains are running there is a second morning departure from Aberystwyth around lunch time, and another in the late afternoon, with the last departure from Devil's Bridge at around tea time. The service starts in early April and continues until late October.

The fares are extremely competitive, with special rates for OAPs, and very favourable fares for accompanying children. There is also a small supplement to travel in the extra splendour of First Class, and this includes the excellent views to be obtained from the observation car at the end of the train. And on the return journey, the locomotive can be seen at close quarters. As well as this special rates are available for parties and School children visits

Intending passengers are of course, advised to check before travelling, and details will be found both at the station itself, and in leaflets freely available around Aberystwyth. Enquiries can also be made to the railway at

Park Avenue,
Aberystwyth,
Credigion,
SY23 1PG

Tel: 01970 625819
Fax: 01970 623769.

www.rheidolrailway.co.uk

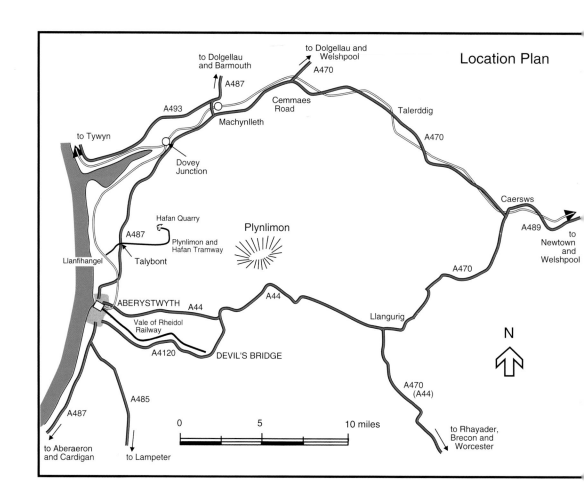

Location Plan

Here is locomotive No 9, in its smart red livery at Devil's Bridge, having just arrived with a train in May 2001. This picture shows well the air brake equipment, and the immaculate condition the engines are kept in.

The afternoon train loading up ready to depart from Aberystwyth on 30 May 2001, locomotive NO 9 PRINCE of WALES in charge, with a semi-open coach as the first vehicle.

A illustration to show something of the Phyllis Rampton Narrow Gauge Railway Trust's work. This little locomotive has been recently restored to an as built and working condition, by Trustee Allen Civil. It was built by Kerr, Stuart & Company Limited, of Stoke-on-Trent, in 1918, for the Ministry of Munitions, and is of the maker's 'Wren' class. Cylinders are 6" diameter and 9" stroke. It came into the Trust's ownership after a long and varied history in the contracting industry, and in a pretty deplorable and dilapidated condition.

Introduction to the Railway: A Brief History

The Vale of Rheidol Railway, with a length a little less than 12 miles, runs from the Welsh coastal town of Aberystwyth, home of the University of Wales, eastwards along the valley of the Afon (River) Rheidol, to Devil's Bridge, raising in the process from but 14 feet above sea level to no less than 680 feet above. To achieve this climb, the last four miles or so are at an average gradient of 1 in 50. Built to the narrow track gauge of 1' 11½", it dates from 22 December 1902, when the first public passenger trains ran, although goods services predated this by some five months or so. Of course, the scheming and building of the line goes back much earlier, and the Act of Parliament under which it was built is dated 6 August 1897, and whilst it was always the intention to carry passengers, timber and the output of the lead mines in the valley were always considered as equally important. Once open, the business generated exceeded all expectations, both passenger and goods, and the Rheidol lead mine, which was on the opposite, north side of the valley to the railway and near Rhiwfron, built an aerial ropeway to get its minerals to the railway. There was also a branch to serve the harbour at Aberystwyth, as well as exchange sidings with the main line railways. By use of these facilities goods and minerals brought down the valley by the railway could be easily transhipped to the main line railways or ships moored in the harbour.

Railways had however, arrived at Aberystwyth much earlier than this, the Aberystwyth & Welsh Coast Railway opened its line to the town on 1 August 1864, followed by the Manchester & Milford Railway on 12 August 1867. The latter railway incidentally, went to neither Manchester or Milford, but it had grandiose plans! It did nevertheless form a junction at Pencader with another line connecting it to Milford Haven. The Aberystwyth & Welsh Coast eventually became a part of the Cambrian Railways in 1865, but the Manchester & Milford remained independent until much later, being absorbed by the Great Western Railway (GWR) in 1911. So, after the opening of the Vale of Rheidol Aberystwyth had no less than three separate railway companies serving its needs. Today, two of them survive, the former Aberystwyth & Welsh Coast is a part of the Network Rail (formerly Railtrack) system and is operated by Wales & Borders Trains, part of the National Express Group, and of course the Vale of Rheidol, the subject of this book. The former Manchester & Milford was a victim of the 'Beeching' cuts, and closed in February 1965.

And so the railway went about its business in a profitable way, the original fleet of three locomotives, one of which it had acquired second hand from the contractor's who built the line, 17 passenger carriages (12 closed and five open), two brake vans and a whole array of goods wagons served it well. There were a number of stations on the line, including two with facilities for trains heading up the valley to cross those coming down and these were at Capel Bangor, four and a half miles from Aberystwyth, and Aberffrwd seven and a half miles from Aberystwyth. As traffic built up several small halts were opened to serve the local populace, and the railway effectively put the local road transport out of business! And as well as this there was much traffic in connection with various army camps situated near the line, both Regular Army and Territorial, and the wonderful views to be had of the valley soon attracted the tourists in the Spring, Summer and Autumn months. The Vale of Rheidol Railway became a reasonably profitable concern regularly returning a dividend of around 3%, but in 1910, the principal shareholders sold out their shares to their big neighbour, the Cambrian Railways, and this turned out to be but a prelude to that

Locomotive No 2 PRINCE of WALES, in is original and elegant livery, seen here at Aberystwyth on 30 June 1909. Notice the good supply of coal and the driver with his oil can, crouching on the front buffer beam. (Late Ken Nunn, Collection Locomotive Club of Great Britain)

Two of the original locomotives seen here at Devil's Bridge in 1921 and after the railway had been acquired by the Cambrian Railways - note its name on the tank sides. The locomotive in front is No 1, formerly EDWARD VII, and the one behind the much smaller RHEIDOL, and they are seen here running round their train prior to the return journey to Aberystwyth. It must have been a heavy train to require two locomotives. Notice by comparing this with the early view on page 6, locomotive No1 has had its coal bunkers extended outwards to increase their capacity. This was done at some time during the First World War, and was partly to compensate for a poorer quality of coal available, the engines needing more of it to get from Aberystwyth to Devil's Bridge and back!

This is the much smaller locomotive RHEIDOL, built by WG Bagnall Limited of Stafford in 1897, originally for a sugar plantation in Brazil but never delivered, instead it worked for a few years on the nearby Plylimon & Hafan Tramway. This tramway served a stone quarry, and on closure this small engine passed to Pethick Brothers, who were the contractor's building the Vale of Rheidol Railway, and hence came into the ownership of the Railway. Notice that like EDWARD V11, she too has lost her name, and acquired the legend Cambrian Railways painted on the tank sides. Picture taken outside the locomotive shed at Aberystwyth in 1921.

This picture shows the second terminus at Aberystwyth, built by the GWR in 1923, to make interchange of passengers between main line and narrow gauge easier. Two trains are seen here ready to depart, one of course, would have to wait until the first reached Aberffrwd before it could leave. Engine No 9 is on the left and No 7 on the right, in this June 1954 photograph, taken before the engines were named.

Company acquiring the Vale of Rheidol Railway on and from 6 July 1913. The big company nevertheless, needed an Act of Parliament to achieve this, so the little railway went down fighting, so to speak!

So started another chapter in the history of the railway, and one, which initially augured well, and because of the greater capital potential behind the Cambrian, many improvements were planned. However, the commencement of hostilities against

country, into four large groups - colloquiall[y] known as 'The Big Four' - under the terms o[f] the Railways Act 1921. Thus the Cambria[n] Railways, and with it the Vale of Rheido[l] became a part of the Great Western Railwa[y] (GWR) from 1 January 1922.

The Great Western was a very progressiv[e] company, indeed it was the only one of 'Th[e] Big Four' to have existed prior to th[e] 'Grouping', as it was called, havin[g] 'absorbed' a whole plethora of smalle[r] railways including th[e] Cambrian, rather tha[n] being formed new as wa[s] the case with the othe[r] three. It wasted littl[e] time therefore, is gettin[g] acquainted with it[s] acquisitions and soo[n] recognised the touris[t] potential of the little Val[e] of Rheidol. The lin[e] needed much spending on it, but neverthele[ss] work was soon underway[,] track was renewed[,] stations refurbished, and a completely new one was built at Aberystwyth alongside the mai[n] line station to better facilitate interchange traffic, the original station being some distance away. A major investment in new locomotives was made too, three being built to augment and part replace the original ones, two in 1923, and a third the following year. However, all was not well on the goods traffic side, most of the mines had closed, and what traffic remained gradually transferred to road such that regular goods services ceased on and from 1 January 1927. Local passenger traffic was suffering from road competition too, a reversal from the railway's earlier days, and regular passenger services ceased on and from 1 January 1931. Thereafter, the line was entirely dependent on the tourist, during the spring, summer and early autumn months, with a complete close down between times. But tourist traffic exceeded all expectations, such that the Great Western made yet further investments having as far back as 1923, supplied four new semi-open sided coaches for use in the high summer, and thus give even better views for passengers of the Rheidol valley. Then, in time for the 1938 season a further three semi-open sided vehicles were built, along with nine new closed coaches - in some cases parts of the original vehicles, under frames and 'running gear' - were used in building

No 8, awaiting to depart from the second terminus at Aberystwyth and taken at the same time as the previous view, June 1954, notice the British Railway crest on the tank side of the locomotive and that at this period, the locomotive did not have a name.

Germany with the onset of the Great War, as it became known, prevented very much being achieved. Clearly a small offshoot of a bigger railway received short shrift in the distribution of funding during the war years, and as well as severe curtailment of the passenger services the infrastructure and rolling stock were allowed to deteriorate, and in some cases get into quite appalling

Locomotive No 8, LLYWELYN, outside the old locomotive shed at Aberystwyth, a photograph taken some time in the 1960s, when the engines sported the smart BR green livery, normally reserved for express locomotives. (Collection Kevin Lane)

condition, despite the heavy traffic from the mines. On cessation of hostilities with the Armistice in November 1918, the following summer the tourists returned, albeit initially in small numbers, and some minor improvements were undertaken to enable the railway to cater for them. But change was in the air again, and agitation by the trades unions which were beginning to flex their muscles, resulted in the grouping of the majority of independent railways in this

he new vehicles. After this investment the entire passenger vehicle fleet was to all intents and purposes new, and specifically designed to allow passengers to get the best possible views of the countryside as they travelled on the line.

Of course, with tourism the only traffic on the onset of the Second World War, the railway closed down completely at the end of the 1939 season, and remained so for the duration of hostilities. But it was looked after, the engines were greased up and left in their shed, and the coaches were sheeted over, and anti deterioration maintenance was undertaken during the entire period of shut down. As we have already seen much track relaying had been undertaken by the GWR soon after it acquired the line, and because of this, and the preventative maintenance that had been undertaken on the rolling stock by enthusiastic local staff, it was possible to reopen the line in its entirety on 23 July 1945. This was just in time for the first intrepid tourists that found there way once again, to this beautiful part of Mid Wales.

Of course, as is now well known , the return of a Labour Government after the war, bent on nationalisation of public services resulted in nationalisation of the railways of this country under the terms of the Transport Act 1947, and the Great Western Railway ceased to exist on and from 1 January 1948. Together with the Vale of Rheidol Railway, the GWR became part of the Western Region of British Railways (BR), but other than that life went on much as before, with the railway providing a service for tourists during the spring, summer and early autumn periods each year. For quite a few years thereafter, business continued to be brisk, and permanent way, buildings and rolling stock were kept in good condition, regularly overhauled and generally looked after. But things were not going well for railways as a whole in the British economy, and in 1963 the 'Beeching' report on the future of railways in this country was published. Dr Richard Beeching had been appointed Chairman of the British Railways Board (A body corporate under the terms of the Railway Act 1962, it replaced the British Transport Commission) some time earlier, with a remit to take a fundamental review of

the entire system, and traffic potential going forwards. The report recommended some extremely fundamental changes, with mass closures of any un-remunerative branch lines and all sorts of other issues that need

not detain us here. Suffice to say, the Vale of Rheidol survived the onslaught, albeit with a curtailment of its facilities, for example the passing loops were removed. Thereafter, only one train could run on the line at any one time, and once a train had left Aberystwyth another one could not leave until the first one had been to Devil's Bridge and back - this made train operation very restrictive. Later, on 15 July 1963, together with all the surviving former Cambrian Railways lines the Vale of Rheidol was transferred from Western Region of BR to the London Midland Region, as a part of a wide sweeping re-organisation.

Despite this change of jurisdiction it was getting increasingly difficult to make a case

to keep the line open, it barely covered its operating expenses let alone capital investment, which was becoming essential. All number of economies were undertaken by the very enthusiastic local and HQ management, including not a few subterfuges to 'cook the books', so to speak. Locomotives and coaches were repaired on

Locomotive No 7 heading up the valley on the new route opened in May 1968, and past the shed and workshops. It is the 1415 train on 8 April 1969, and shows the locomotive in the BR 'corporate' Rail Blue livery, the coaches being in the same colours too.
(C. C. Green)

Trains on their way up the valley now take water at Nantyronen, as the supply there is more reliable than Aberffrwd, and here is No 8 doing so with the first train of the season (notice the very light train) in March 2001. The Fireman can be seen manipulating the hose pipe into the engine's water tank.

site rather then sent away to Main Workshops, with their high overhead recovery requirements, and when in need of higher levels of repair they were taken to Regional Workshops, when it was possible to 'loose' overheads! In September 1966, the Chester Division of the London Midland Region of which the railway was a part of, was absorbed by the Stoke-on-Trent Division, and thus the railway came under the management of the late George Dow, who was the Divisional Manager there at the time and a great enthusiast, so that support

A short pause at Aberffrwd for locomotive No 8, with an up train on 16 April 1998. When trains pass each other here, those heading up the valley use the other, right hand track.

of the line was not only maintained, but also increased. Indeed George Dow was able to get authority for a relatively expensive scheme, to divert the line at the Aberystwyth end into the then otherwise redundant bay of the main line station formerly used by the Camarthen trains - a route closed under the 'Beeching' proposals. This not only shortened the route somewhat, obviating a rather circuitous route by the river, but it also made redundant a rather troublesome level crossing, and made interchange of passengers between main line and narrow gauge even more convenient. As well as this, the former main line locomotive shed, also redundant with the demise of main line steam locomotives, became available and this was converted into a narrow gauge combined locomotive shed, workshop and carriage shed. This shed dates from 1938, although it is on the site of an earlier shed dating from 1864, when it was opened by the Aberystwyth & Welsh Coast Railway. For almost the first time in the line's history, significant numbers of passenger rolling stock could be stored under cover, a boom in the winter months.

By this time the line was becoming something of an icon and as steam was gradually eliminated from the main line railways, the little Vale of Rheidol was destined to become the last remaining use of steam locomotives by British Railways - did anybody dare close it now! And so the

railway soldiered on for a few more years but long-term maintenance was being neglected, safety was not being compromised, but the gradual infrastructure renewal that is essential to keep long-term assets viable was lacking. Some improvements were made however, in attempts to increase revenue, stations were spruced up, locomotives were painted different colours, and special events were organised. Arrangements were also made for more than one train to operate at any one time, by a second train following the first up the valley after the former had reached Nantyronen, and onwards after the first one had got to Devil's Bridge. They then returned by the same procedure, and whilst this was not as convenient as passing en route, it did significantly increase capacity and could be accomplished with little extra expenditure, and without the additional staff required to man a passing loop.

Notwithstanding all that was achieved during this period, the Government of the day were determined to gradually take away from British Railway's control its various subsidiaries and ancillary operations, and this ideal finally reached the little Vale of Rheidol, and it was placed on the market as a going concern in 1988. Eventually, after a lot of interest the railway was sold as a going concern to a private partnership in 1989 and as a result became the first part of the British Railway's railway system, as opposed to ancillary undertakings, to return to private enterprise. It was a strict condition of sale that the buyer had to illustrate its ability to continue to operate the railway, and this ruled out a number of the bidders who it was felt, lacked the financial backing to achieve this. The railway is now owned by a Charitable Trust, and is operated as a completely independent narrow gauge railway, for the pleasure of all who want to make the wonderful scenic journey up the River Rheidol valley, as has been the case for over 100 years. Unlike most of the other surviving narrow gauge railways in Wales, the Vale of Rheidol is manned entirely by paid staff; there are no volunteers. The Trust's Trustees are of course, unpaid and devote their time and effort freely for the furtherance of the Trust's objectives, in continuing to see this wonderful little railway survive and prosper, thus supporting not only the railway heritage of this country, but also enabling people from all walks of life the opportunity of enjoying this uniquely beautiful part of Wales.

Since the railway has passed into private ownership much has been achieved. It has to be said, it had been allowed by BR to fall into a pretty run down state, and it is extremely doubtful it could have carried on running much longer without the major investment that has been possible since its sale. During the last few years the entire main line has been re-laid with new rail and sleepers, in many cases the rail is of a heavier section than hitherto, so it should require little major attention for a good many years subject to normal routine maintenance. At Llanbadarn, one mile from Aberystwyth the line crosses the Afon Rheidol by a six arch timber trestle bridge, but due to rot in the timbers, this bridge had to be completely renewed during the winter of 1991-2. But the Trustees and local management are not complacent, and with a railway such as this, with a formation one hundred years old, one never knows what might be required next!

Two of the locomotives, No 8 and No 9, have been extensively rebuilt at the workshops of the Brecon Mountain Railway; they had already been converted to oil, rather than coal firing by BR in 1978. This latter makes their operation much cleaner, and less labour intensive. The third locomotive, No 7, whilst it too has been converted to oil firing has otherwise only had minimal work undertaken on it, and is currently dismantled for a similar level of repair to its sisters. All the coaches have had work undertaken on them to some extent or other, and in some cases this has been an extensive rebuild. The entire fleet of locomotives and 12 of the 16 existing passenger coaches have been converted to use the automatic air brake, hitherto the trains were vacuum braked which was a far less effective system and more expensive to maintain. The most obvious evidence of this change is the compressed air steam pump mounted on the right hand side in front of the side tanks on the locomotives, and its distinctive intermittent exhaust through the locomotive chimney, even when the locomotive is not moving. All of the surviving goods vehicles have also been renovated, and are used to assist with maintenance trains for the track and other parts of the infrastructure. Some additional vehicles have also been added, as well as 'on track' machinery to ease the maintenance burden of the track and formation .

The passing loop at Aberffrwd has been reinstated and trains regularly pass there in the mid summer months when there are two trains operating, and in addition the loop at Capel Bangor has also been replaced, and now the railway is operated in three sections. However, presently passenger trains do not normally pass at Capel Bangor, but engineering trains are frequently recessed there to allow passenger trains to pass them. At Devil's Bridge a small café and shop has been erected, and to improve the views of the valley large acreages of forest have been acquired, and some tree lopping and felling has been undertaken, as well as it has to said, some replanting. There is much more work needed in this direction if we are again to get all the breathtaking views enjoyed by our forbearers. Considerable improvements have been made at Aberystwyth itself, in particular car-parking facilities.

The Trust that owns the line has also been busy acquiring other locomotives and rolling stock, some of which can been seen around the station area. It is hoped one day to restore these to working order, both for occasional use on the line and display in a museum to be built adjacent to the railway in Aberystwyth. Improvements to the passenger facilities at both Aberystwyth and Devil's Bridge, as well as the workshops, locomotive and rolling stock sheds are also planned These are however, rather long-term plans. Other additions have been a number of items of mechanical plant to help with track maintenance. These include a ballast-tamping machine and some special wagons with doors underneath specifically designed to carry and unload track ballast.

Under the terms of the legislation connected with the privatisation of BR, The Railway Heritage Committee was formed. This Committee has powers to designate items of significant historical interest, formerly in the ownership of BR, for preservation, should their existing owners no longer require them. In 1999 the Committee so designated the VoR locomotives and rolling stock, together with some items of infrastructure. Of course, the Trust cannot imagine a time when it no longer wants them, but it is a tremendous boost to it activities to know that they are considered of so much interest, and to such an august body.

The Locomotives

The railway started life with three steam locomotives and as recounted earlier two were new and one came from the contractor who built the line. Dealing first with the new ones, these were of the 2-6-2 wheel arrangement, that is a pair of carrying

the Great Western Railway accounts as a 'rebuild' to enable the costs to allocated t revenue, rather than capital account. Th old locomotive was in fact scrapped, and a new one constructed in its place, eventuall becoming No 9 in the fleet.

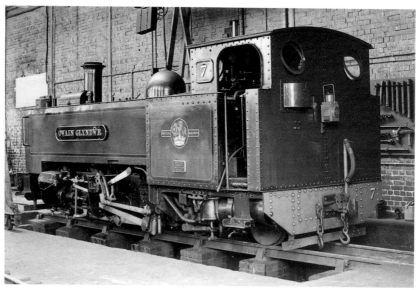

A view of No 7 OWAIN GLYNDWR, in the former main line locomotive shed at Aberystwyth in July 1987. The engine was then running in the British Railways express steam locomotive green livery, with the later crest, although by this time the railway had been sold. It was still vacuum braked at this time, notice the large diameter pipe on the buffer beam, and the large brake cylinder which can just be seen in front of the cab footstep.

The third of th original engines wa much smaller, being o the 2-4-0 whee arrangement and dating from 1896 Built by WG Bagnal Limited of Stafford, i had originally beer intended for use on a sugar plantation in Brazil, but had beer diverted to the nearby Plynlimon & Hafar Tramway; a line serving lead mine north of Aberystwyth Then, after this line

wheels at each end, and six driven ones in the middle, and were tank engines carrying their water supply in large tanks each side of the boiler. They were built by Messrs Davies & Metcalfe of Romiley near Stockport in 1902, and became No 1 EDWARD VII and No 2 PRINCE of WALES, opening of the railway having taken place of course, shortly after the Coronation of Edward VII. These were it seems the only locomotives ever built by this company, but the Davies's of Davies & Metcalfe were from Aberystwyth, maintained interests in the locality, and were among the promoters of the railway. In any event, they were well built and sturdy machines, and with few alterations worked the bulk of the traffic, requiring them both to be in use on most weekdays, for over 20 years. Their two cylinders were 11" diameter and 17" stroke, the driving wheels were 2'6" diameter, the boiler pressure 150 psi, and the weight in working order 22 tons. As mentioned earlier, on takeover by the GWR both these engines were eventually replaced, in the case of No 1 which became GWR No 1212, it was removed from the line in 1932, and scrapped in 1935. Its sister however, which became GWR No 1213, was ostensibly rebuilt to conform exactly to the same characteristics as the new engines supplied in 1923, but in fact this was not the case. The 'rebuilt' locomotive was shown in

ceased operations on closure of the mines, i passed via its maker's to the contractor' Pethick Brothers, who had the contract to build the Vale of Rheidol line, and subsequently via them it came into the Railway's ownership. Named RHEIDOL although much smaller than its counterpart it proved useful with, for example, the lightly loaded early morning train, and for assisting the other engines when loads were heavy. I had cylinders 8" diameter and 12" stroke driving wheels 2'3" diameter, a boiler pressure of 140 psi, and the weight in working order equalled 13 tons. Once the new engines arrived in 1923, little RHEIDOL was taken out of service and scrapped in the following year.

The three new engines were all built by the GWR at its Swindon Works in Wiltshire. In principle they were very similar to the original engines, retaining the successful characteristics whilst improving the less successful; the wheel arrangement and water tank configuration was the same. Among the principal improvements was the arrangement of the valve gear, and this was placed completely outside the frames making maintenance much easier. Main dimensions were the same except the cylinder diameter with half an inch larger, the boiler pressure was higher and the weight in working order went up to 25 tons. They were therefore, more powerful than the original engines but as mentioned above retained all their good points. In service they have proved extremely successful and can handle with ease fully loaded seven coach trains on the steepest gradients, and even in adverse weather conditions. In 1956 these three locomotives were given the fully lined out green livery reserved by BR for its express passenger locomotives, and had names bestowed on them. No 7 became OWAIN GLYNDWR, No 8 LLYWELYN, and No 9 PRINCE of WALES. This last name was of course, the name of the engine that No 9 was ostensibly 'rebuilt' from - a nice touch by the authorities. Currently it retains its name and sports a nice maroon livery, whilst No 8 is running without its name and in the GWR plain green livery of the 1930s period. The third locomotive is, as mentioned earlier currently dismantled for a heavy overhaul.

The diesel locomotive, which has taken the next number in the list - No 10 - came to the line shortly before the sale by British Railways. It should be added, that the numerical sequence of the steam locomotives, 7 to 9, was part of a wider GWR and later BR scheme, as they were numbered as a part of the entire GWR and later BR fleet. No 10 has an 0-6-0 wheel arrangement, that is six driven wheels only, with a Caterpillar 165 horse power engine and a hydraulic transmission. It was built in the workshops of the Brecon Mountain Railway at Pant in 1987, from parts acquired from the liquidation sale of Baguley-Drewry Limited, the Burton-on-Trent based firm of locomotive and railway engineers who went 'bust' about that time. It can often be seen going about its 'normal' duties hauling maintenance trains at one or other of the passing loops, otherwise it will be found at the depot in Aberystwyth. In emergencies it can however, haul passenger trains.

Another view in Aberystwyth locomotive shed in July 1987, this time showing locomotive No 9 PRINCE of WALES, and at that time painted in an approximation of the livery it carried when new, Oxford yellow-ochre. This was the same colour the London Brighton & South Coast Railway painted its locomotives, and it seems one of the original Director's liked it, and managed to obtain supplies from that Railway Company! The vacuum pipe is again prominent on the buffer beam - compare this with pictures taken later, after the locomotives were converted to air brakes.

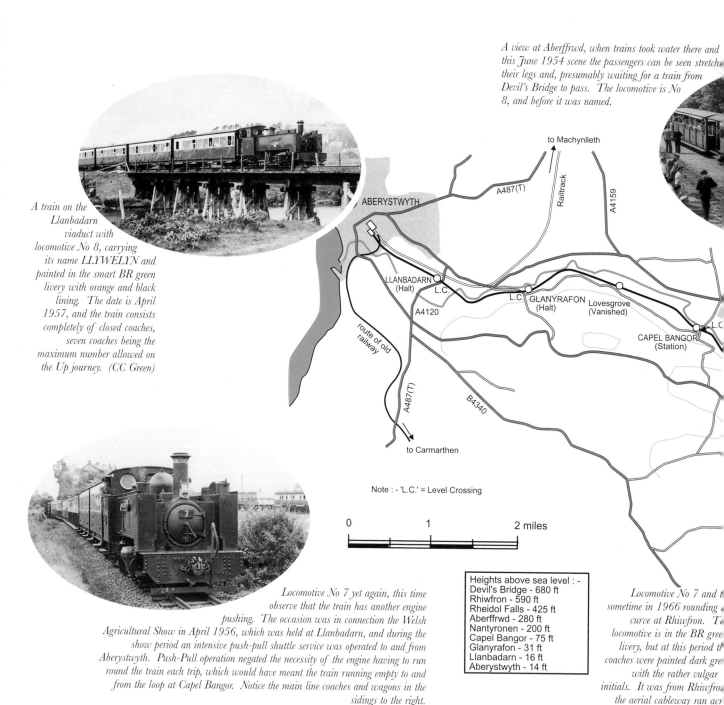

A view at Aberffrwd, when trains took water there and ... this June 1954 scene the passengers can be seen stretch... their legs and, presumably waiting for a train from Devil's Bridge to pass. The locomotive is No 8, and before it was named.

A train on the Llanbadarn viaduct with locomotive No 8, carrying its name LLYWELYN and painted in the smart BR green livery with orange and black lining. The date is April 1957, and the train consists completely of closed coaches, seven coaches being the maximum number allowed on the Up journey. (CC Green)

to Machynlleth

A487(T)

Railtrack

A4159

ABERYSTWYTH

LLANBADARN (Halt)   L.C.

L.C.   GLANYRAFON (Halt)

Lovesgrove (Vanished)

L.C.

CAPEL BANGOR (Station)

A4120

route of old railway

A487(T)

B4340

to Carmarthen

Note : - 'L.C.' = Level Crossing

0   1   2 miles

Heights above sea level : -
Devil's Bridge - 680 ft
Rhiwfron - 590 ft
Rheidol Falls - 425 ft
Aberffrwd - 280 ft
Nantyronen - 200 ft
Capel Bangor - 75 ft
Glanyrafon - 31 ft
Llanbadarn - 16 ft
Aberystwyth - 14 ft

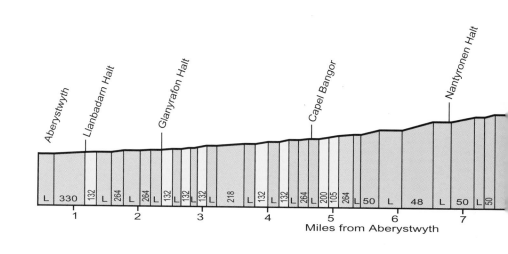

Locomotive No 7 yet again, this time observe that the train has another engine pushing. The occasion was in connection the Welsh Agricultural Show in April 1956, which was held at Llanbadarn, and during the show period an intensive push-pull shuttle service was operated to and from Aberystwyth. Push-Pull operation negated the necessity of the engine having to run round the train each trip, which would have meant the train running empty to and from the loop at Capel Bangor. Notice the main line coaches and wagons in the sidings to the right.

Locomotive No 7 and ... sometime in 1966 rounding ... curve at Rhiwfron. T... locomotive is in the BR gree... livery, but at this period t... coaches were painted dark gre... with the rather vulgar ... initials. It was from Rhiwfro... the aerial cableway ran acr... valley to the Cwmrheidol Min... bringing the minerals to the r... for onward transport to Aberys... (CC ...

Gradient Profile

Aberystwyth

Llanbadarn Halt

Glanyrafon Halt

Capel Bangor

Nantyronen Halt

| L | 330 | 132 | L | 264 | L | 264 | L | 132 | L | 132 | L | 132 | L | 218 | L | 132 | L | 132 | L | 264 | 200 | 105 | 264 | L | 50 | L | 48 | L | 50 | L | 50 |

1   2   3   4   5   6   7

Miles from Aberystwyth

RAILWAY COMPA...

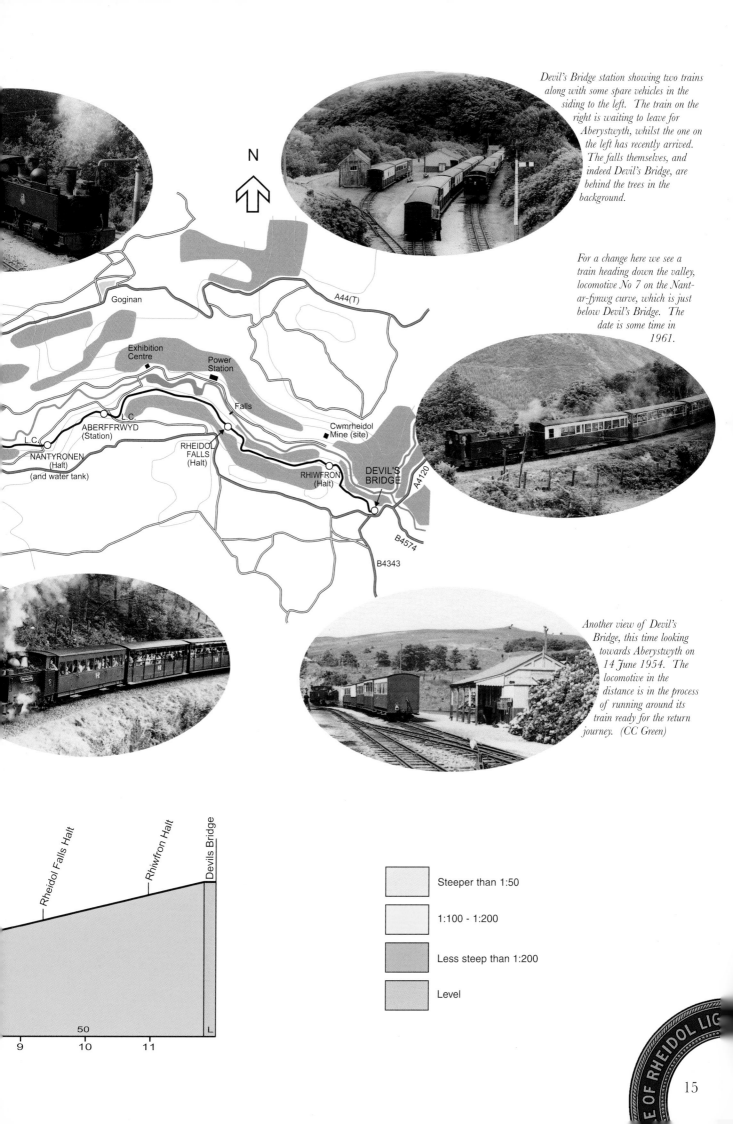

Devil's Bridge station showing two trains along with some spare vehicles in the siding to the left. The train on the right is waiting to leave for Aberystwyth, whilst the one on the left has recently arrived. The falls themselves, and indeed Devil's Bridge, are behind the trees in the background.

For a change here we see a train heading down the valley, locomotive No 7 on the Nant-ar-fynwg curve, which is just below Devil's Bridge. The date is some time in 1961.

Another view of Devil's Bridge, this time looking towards Aberystwyth on 14 June 1954. The locomotive in the distance is in the process of running around its train ready for the return journey. (CC Green)

N

Goginan

A44(T)

Exhibition Centre

Power Station

Falls

L.C.

ABERFFRWYD (Station)

Cwmrheidol Mine (site)

L.C.

NANTYRONEN (Halt)
(and water tank)

RHEIDOL FALLS (Halt)

RHIWFRON (Halt)

DEVIL'S BRIDGE

A4120

B4574

B4343

Rheidol Falls Halt

Rhiwfron Halt

Devils Bridge

50

L

9   10   11

Steeper than 1:50

1:100 - 1:200

Less steep than 1:200

Level

Rolling Stock

The passenger carrying rolling stock consists of 16 bogie coaches, nine of which are closed and the reminder with open sides. Apart from a few under frames and parts of 'running gear', they all date from either 1923 or 1938 and were built by the GWR at its Swindon Workshops in Wiltshire. Numbers 13-16, semi-open type were built to Lot No 1333 of 1923, and were originally GWR and BR numbers 4997-5000; of these No 15 was converted in 1983 to a 'Vista' car. Numbers 1-6 and 10, closed type were built to Lot No 1615 of 1938, and were originally GWR and BR numbers 4143-48/94, and at the same time Lot 1618 covered three semi-open coaches numbers 7-9, formerly GWR and BR numbers 4148-51. Two closed coaches with brake/guards compartments were built in 1938 to Lot No 1616, numbers 11-12,

formerly GWR and BR numbers 4995-6; these two were converted to observation cars, with end windows in 1983-4, but retained their brake/guards compartments. Most of these coaches have been completely rebuilt in recent years, or at the very least had much time and effort spent on improving them. There is also one GWR built four wheel brake van surviving out of three that were built in 1938 to Lot No 1617, GWR and BR numbers 135-7. The survivor is number 19 in the fleet, and is used when it is necessary to run three passenger trains simultaneously. As noted above, with only two of the bogie coaches equipped with brake compartments for the guard to undertake his duties, this brake van has to be attached to any third train in operation.

Locomotive No 7, OWAIN GLYNDWR, just before it was dismantled for extensive repairs in 1998. Notice nevertheless, it is in immaculate condition.

For a time No 8 ran in the plain black livery it would have carried had it ever been in Cambrian Railways ownership, and here it is thus painted outside the locomotive shed at Aberystwyth in July 1987.

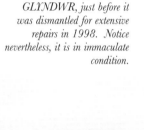

Locomotive No 9 PRINCE of WALES, illustrated here taking on water at Aberystwyth in May 2001. Notice in comparison with earlier views - page 13 is a good comparison - the addition of the air brake pump in front of the right hand water tank. Also that the cab roof has been modified slightly to give a more heard room for the crew. When they were built the overall height of the engines was restricted by an overbridge on the original route of the line which ran near the harbour, but as this restriction no longer applies, the opportunity was taken during the recent heavy overhauls to modify this locomotive and No 8.

The three locomotives have Walschaerts valve gear, and this photograph taken in April 1988, illustrates the gear in close up on locomotive No 8. Note that because of the narrow track gauge, the wheels are inside the frames, the leaf springs for which can just be discerned above. Walschaert was a Belgian, who invented this form of valve gear, one of the most successful ever used on steam locomotives.

One of the semi-open coaches - as they are referred to - this one is No 13 built at Swindon in 1923, heavily rebuilt by the Railway in recent years, and seen here having just received attention in the Paint Shop.

One of the closed coaches outside the shed at Aberystwyth, this is No 1, built at Swindon in 1938.

The only three remaining five plank open wagons that came to the railway from the Plynimon & Hafan Tramway. The contractor who built the Vale of Rheidol Railway purchased these wagons from the closed Tramway, and used them on the construction works, and they later passed into the ownership of the Railway itself. Although much rebuilt over the years, they date originally from 1897, and are a treasured part of the rolling stock, as can be seen by the excellent condition they are kept in. As seen here they are loaded with ballast for use on the line.

The sole remaining brake van, No 19 built at Swindon in 1938 and extensively rebuilt at Aberystwyth, where this picture was taken in December 2002.

The Baguley-Drewry diesel locomotive No 10, hauling one of the flat wagons converted from an open wagon, and four of the four plank open wagons, on a 'works' train leaving Aberystwyth to do 'business' on the line in December 2002. The large building behind is the locomotive and rolling stock shed and workshop - the former main line locomotive shed.

Here we see the two ex South African Railways bogie ballast wagons, as converted for use on the railway. Needless to say, with their bottom discharge doors they are extremely useful to the maintenance teams.

There are also 14 vehicles of non passenger carrying rolling stock, some of which date from 1897, and were used by the contractor building the line, but had also been in use even before that date, like the early locomotive RHEIDOL, on the nearby Plynlimon & Hafan Tramway. There are six of these, four wheel vehicles of five ton carrying capacity and originally with five plank sides and obviously much rebuilt over the years. Three of them have been converted to flat wagons - and the six carry the numbers 25-30. A further five wagons dating from 1906 survive, also four wheel and of five ton carrying capacity, but this time with four plank sides. Numbered 20-24, one of these has also been cut down to a flat wagon. Three more wagons have been added in recent years, numbers 31-33, one is actually a four bogie bolster 'set', extensively rebuilt by the Railway from some old wagons purchased from Bowater's Paper Mill in Kent; it is used for moving rail. The other two are bogie ballast hoppers that came from South Africa, and they too, have been extensively rebuilt by the Railway and fitted with air brakes. Presently all these vehicles are used for track and infrastructure maintenance purposes.

In addition there is a self propelled 'Permaquip inspection vehicle and equipment trolley, and a 'Plasser' ballast tamper that was built in, and formerly used in South Africa.

A Trip up the Line

The journey starts in the former Manchester & Milford Railway bay platform at Aberystwyth station, and because of the height difference between the narrow gauge train and a main line one, we don't board from the platform, but from ground level on the opposite side. On leaving the train passes the former main line locomotive shed dating from 1939, and which now serves the needs of the narrow gauge railway. In general terms the line is uphill all the way to Devil's Bridge, although the real slog does not commence until Capel Bangor, some four and a half miles away. Soon we come to Llanbadarn, where along with the main line railway to Shrewsbury, the line crosses the Llanbadarn to Aberaeron road on the level, the A 4120. The main line level crossing has automatic barriers whilst the Vale of Rheidol one does not, and although independent arrangements exist, because of the short roadway between the two level crossings, when two trains approach simultaneously, one has to wait for the other. This is to stop road vehicles getting trapped between the two crossings, and their drivers being tempted to zig-zag through the half barriers. Hence,

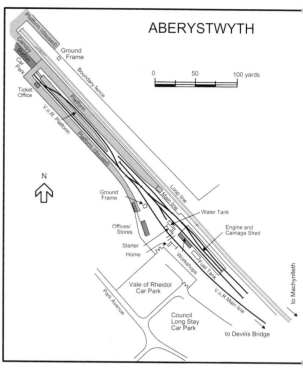

ABERYSTWYTH

onwards past Llanbadarn (25' above sea level) to where the line crosses the Afon Rheidol by a six arch timber trestle bridge, the largest structure on the entire railway. During the construction period of the railway, ballast from the river bed here was used, and there was a siding for this purpose.

Shortly after passing over the river we come to a very modern Glanyrafon industrial estate on the right hand side, and automatic barriers control the busy level crossing, similar to those we have just passed and used for the main line railway. There is a small Halt here, and this is about the termination of urban life as we make our way up the valley, and hereafter it is very much a country railway. The line continues from here with slightly adverse gradients but with

In contrast to the pictures on page 16, here is locomotive No 7 at Aberystwyth in September 1971, and illustrating the somewhat run down condition at that time. Notice the extra coal on top of the bunker, and on the cab floor.

whichever train, main line or narrow gauge, gets to the trigger point first, has the clear road, whilst the other has to stop and wait. It is pretty easy going, and relatively flat

Locomotive No 7 again, this time heading up the valley on the original line that ran near the harbour, with the Afon Rheidol on the left and the old locomotive shed behind the train. A photograph taken in 1961 by the late CC Green, a prolific historian of the Railway.

everal short stretches on the level, and there are numerous views of the river on the left hand side, together with very fertile farmland. At Capel Bangor four and a half miles and still but 75 feet above sea level, we find the recently reinstated passing loop, which is extremely useful if the maintenance train is working on the lower section of the line on the day we travel. Long ago there was a carriage shed situated here on the left hand side, and where coaches were kept in the winter months. The siding that served this shed has also been reinstated, but no shed - yet!

From Capel Banger, the village by the way, or perhaps more accurately described as a hamlet, is about half a mile distant to the left

(north), and on the main A 44 Trunk road; the line now starts to climb in earnest. During the ensuing three miles to Aberffrwd, with several stretches of 1 in 40-50, interspersed with level sections, the train climbs some 200 feet and it is in the early part of this section that we see the Afon Rheidol at close quarters for the last time. Also, the forest starts to close in around us, with the pinewoods of Tanyrallt on the right hand side. Soon we come to Nantyronen Halt six and three quarter miles and 200 feet above sea level, where there was once a siding, and where splendid views can be had across the Duffryn

Rheidol - here we start to get a true measure of the magnificence of the Vale of the Afon Rheidol. Trains always stop here on the way up the valley, for it is the principle watering

point for the engines and tanks are filled to capacity for the climb ahead. Until 1983 water was only taken at Aberffrwd, but the supply there tended to be less reliable; however, the Cambrian Railways built cast iron water tank survives.

On then to Aberffrwd climbing at 1 in 50 for much of the way and with the river getting further and further below, and some quite marvellous views. At Aberffrwd, seven and half miles and about 280 feet above sea level, is the main passing loop and when two trains are running at the height of the season

A drivers eye view of the viaduct over the Afon Rheidol at Llanbadarn, locomotive No 9 PRINCE of WALES heading up the valley in September 1959. (CC Green)

A September 1959 view of locomotive No 7 and train, at this time the engines were painted in the BR express passenger locomotive green livery, and the coaches in the former GWR chocolate and cream. The train is seen here on its way up the valley having just left the immediate environs of Aberystwyth. Notice to the right wagons in the main line sidings. Another of the late CC Green's photographs.

Here we see a train heading up the valley waiting in the loop at Aberffrwd for one coming down from Devil's Bridge to pass. The locomotive is No 8, in the livery it runs in today and the date 16 April 1998. The first coach is one of the semi-open ones, and notice behind the second coach the old Cambrian Railways water tank.

A view taken by the late CC Green in June 1956, from the north side of the Afon Rheidol, looking up the valley towards Devil's Bridge. Notice the plume of smoke from the train ascending the 1 in 50 gradient between Aberffrwd and Rheidol Falls Halt, in fact the train is almost at the site of the halt, and the course of the line cut into the hill side can be clearly followed, disappearing for a part of the view as it rounds the sharp curve at Cwm-yr-ogos (known to the staff as 'Oliver Veltum's' curve). The falls themselves can also be seen on the river at the foot of the valley, directly below the train.

19

whichever one arrives first waits for the other. After leaving there is but a short stretch of level track, which helps the get away, and then it is 1 in 50 all the way to Devil's Bridge, four miles without a break for the engine, but with the most spectacular views for the passengers. Here the train leaves behind the open Duffryn Rheidol and comes across the steep and narrow Cwmrheidol, which is the Rheidol Valley itself. The railway runs on an almost continuous ledge cut out of the side of the mountains and this continues all the way to Devil's Bridge. Looking back glimpses can be had of the Cwm Rheidol Reservoir and the hydro power station, and on the far side of the valley can be seen the remains of the mine workings of years ago, and which was one of the reasons the line was built. The scar left by the mine workings incidentally, is known locally as 'The Stag', notice that it has the appearance of the animal of this name. About here will be seen the site of Rheidol Falls Halt (425' above sea level). Soon the line takes a rather

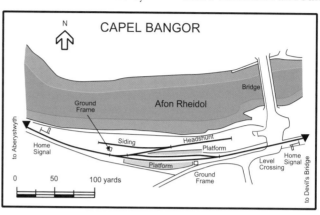

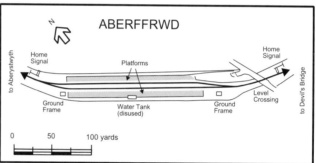

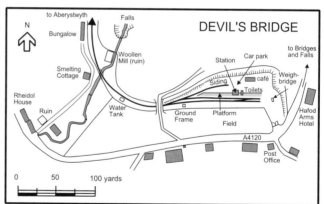

sharp turn to the right and enters the gorge known as Cwm-yr-ogos, meaning Valley of the Caves, and on the right is the site of the former Erwtomau mine. This is generally known as Horseshoe Bend, and more old mine workings can be seen. More woodlands follow and then the site of Rhiwfron Halt, 10¾ miles and about 590 feet above sea level. From here we can see across the valley and the scar on the opposite side of the old Cwmrheidol mine, and it was from

that mine that the aerial ropeway mentioned earlier brought the lead ore to be transhipped by the railway to Aberystwyth.

It is not far now, as the engine continues to work hard against the 1in 50 grade, and soon we round the final curves, pass through a deep cutting and the remains of an old woollen mill, to enter Devil's Bridge station. Here we find a run round loop for the engine and a siding, along with a booking office, café and shop, with picnic facilities and the like. The small village of Devil' Bridge is but a short distance away with a hotel, shop and other amenities. And of course, here are situated the Devil's water fall, which are well worth a visit during the train's stop over or take more time if you decide to return by a later train. Here in the depths of the gorge is the little Afon Mynach tumbling down to reach the Rheidol.

You have now travelled a little over 11 and three quarter miles and climbed 680 feet above sea level, 565 of those feet in the last six and a half miles, and Devil's Bridge itself is 380 feet above the Afon Rheidol; the journey has taken about one hour. If your train was fully loaded with seven coaches, as it is likely to be in high summer and at holiday times, it will have a tare weight of around 50 tons (7 tons per coach), plus the engines weight of 25 tons. A full complement of passengers would equal around another 16 tons, say an gross weight of 90 tons, or 75 tons without the engine. The engine has a tractive effort equal to 10510 lbs at 85% of its 165 psi steam working pressure, which at a speed of say, 15 mph, would equate to an indicated horsepower of 420 on level track. Not bad for a locomotive 80 years old, and when one considers the ruling grade against the engine all the way from Aberffrwd is 1 in 50.

The bridge from which the hamlet of Devil's Bridge takes its name, is in fact three bridges on top of each other. Legend has it that the first bridge here was built by the Devil, hence its name, and it was on the promise that he would 'have' the first soul to cross over it. The legend continues that a dog was sent, and that the Devil was so disgusted that he went away, never to return, leaving the dog to its own devices! The lowest of the three arches is reputed to be one of the oldest stone bridges in the country, and is though to have been built by Monks from Strata Florida Abbey, in the year 1087AD. The middle, or centre arch was erected in 1753, while the top one and the one currently used dates from 1901, when the local County Council built it. The Afon Mynach has under these arches carved a foaming whirlpool, which is known as the Devil's Punchbowl, and from it falls the Mynach some 210 feet on its way to join the Rheidol,

which at this point is some 500 feet below the bridge. William Wordsworth's sonnet, 'The Torrent at Devil's Bridge, has perhaps, done most to make the World aware of this lovely place, although several other famous men have, over the years, admired its beauties, Ruskin and Turner to name but two. When you have taken the time to make the train journey to Devil's Bridge, do not miss the opportunity to witness this amazing spectacle.

A recent view from a passing train of the Cwm Rheidol Reservoir, part of the Llwgn-y-groes pumped storage power generation scheme.

A view taken in August 1963 looking down the valley at the Afon Rheidol from just above Allt-ddu, with the locomotive of an Up train working hard in the foreground. August 1962. (CC Green)

A picture taken just a little bit further up the line from the previous one, at Allt-ddu, and showing the 1430 train from Aberystwyth on 28 August 1983, hauled by locomotive No 7 painted in BR green livery at that time.

A fireman's eye view this time looking up the valley from the sharp curve just above Rhiwfron cutting, locomotive No 7 in June 1956. Until recently this view had been lost due to the extensive Forest of trees hereabouts, but some conservative and necessary felling has made much of it available again. (CC Green)

On a sunny summer day in June 1956, the late CC Green was on the footplate of locomotive No 8, and this is the Fireman's view as the train approaches Rhiwfron.

57016   DEVIL'S BRIDGE TRAIN, VALE OF RHEIDOL RAILWAY.

Commercial postcard of a train on the Horseshoe bend as it is known, which is just short of Devil's Bridge. This card was published by Harvey Barton & Sons Limited of Bristol, and was posted in Aberystwyth on 31 August 1961, to my parents by friends on holiday there. The picture however, is much earlier as it shows the locomotive running without a name, so it dates from around 1954. The engine is No 9, identifiable as this is the engine that ran during that period without its smoke box number plate. Notice the semi - open coach with the side sheets down, it must have been a cold day!

A postcard view of Devil's Bridge on a busy day showing two trains along with some spare vehicles in the siding. These would have been detached from an early Up train, and would be attached again to the last down train of the day, thus catering for those who wanted to spend the day in the locality, and to save hauling too many empty coaches around all day. The card was sent to a friend in Crewe in December 1961, having been posted in York bearing a 2½d (old currency, about one new pence) stamp! Compare these views of Devil's Bridge with the earlier one on page 2, and see how little it altered over the years - a delightful spot and well worth the trip up the line.

Taking water at Devil's Bridge, locomotive No 7 about to head down the valley, as the driver looks on attentively and the fireman attends to the engines needs. The train has just drawn out of the station under the bridge, presumably there was not time for the engine to take water separately. An August 1958 view by the late CC Green.

A train about to leave Devil's Bridge some time in 1966 with locomotive No 9 PRINCE of WALES. Water is available for the engines here, taken from a stream that runs into the Afon Rheidol and situated just beyond the footbridge in the distance, To take water the engines have to run someway under the bridge. (CC Green)

Locomotive No 7 and train waiting to leave Devil's Bridge on 26 August 1959.

Here is No 8 again, this time in GWR green livery and as it would have been painted when built in 1923. It is seen here at Devil's Bridge in April 1998, waiting to return with its train to Aberystwyth. This is the livery the engine appears in today, and without its name.

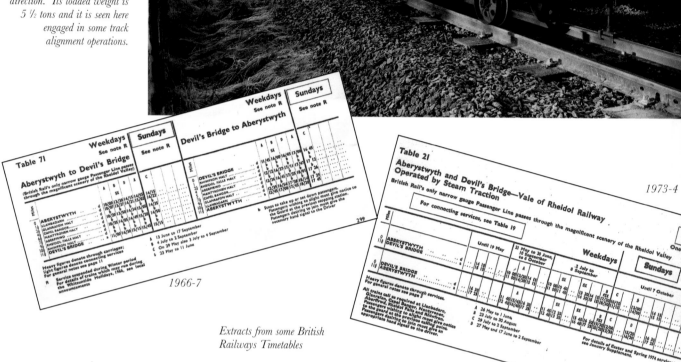

This picture show the 'Permaqup' Trolley used by the track maintenance crews, along with its small trailer. These vehicles were built for BR in 1985, and up to nine people can be carried. Fitted with a four cylinder diesel engine, the trolley itself has an in built hydraulic turntable, so that it can be turned round at any time to face the opposite direction. Its loaded weight is 5 ½ tons and it is seen here engaged in some track alignment operations.

Extracts from some British Railways Timetables

1966-7

1973-4

June-September 1960

An extremely useful item of on-track equipment is this Plasserail ballast tamper, seen here at work on the line - notice the tamping arms digging into the ballast. It was built in 1985 in South Africa, and came to the railway in 1991 having been extensively overhauled by its maker's first. Self propelled it can travel at up to 9 mph, and has a Deutz four cylinder diesel engine rated at 55 horse power. Weighing 4 tons, it can tamp 2 sleepers per minute, and without it it is doubtful if the complete track renewal programme could have been completed yet.

A beautiful setting seen here, against the backdrop of the mountains and in the late summer of 1959, as locomotive No 9 heads up the valley, along the south traverse above Rhiwfron, almost at the last of the horseshoe bends. Another of the late CC Green's views.

SECTION D   86

SECTIONAL APPENDIX TO THE WORKING TIME TABLE AND BOOKS OF RULES AND REGULATIONS—SHREWSBURY TRAFFIC DISTRICT—continued.

Page 198

Vale of Rheidol Branch

Delete the paragraph under the above heading and substitute the following :

Vale of Rheidol Branch
(Narrow Gauge—1 ft. 11½ in.)
WORKING INSTRUCTIONS

During the stipulated Summer period, the Vale of Rheidol Branch Line will be worked by Train Staff and Ticket, such period being announced by special notice.

The Staff, Tickets and Ticket Boxes, which are coloured red, for the line Aberystwyth to Devil's Bridge, will be kept in the signal boxes and the Signalman will be the only person authorised to receive or deliver a Staff or Ticket.

The Staff will be used for working the Ground Frame at Capel Bangor and the Ground Frames to the Transfer Siding and Locomotive and Carriage Siding at Aberystwyth.

At the end of each day, all cancelled tickets must then be forwarded to the Aberystwyth Station Master who will forward them to the District Superintendent at the end of each week. At other times the line will be worked by "One Engine in Steam" regulations.

During the times the line is worked under "One Engine in Steam" regulations, the staff will be kept on the engine in a locked box, the key of which must be kept in the possession of the Driver. The staff in possession of the Driver will be utilised as required to unlock the Ground Frames to gain admission to the various sidings on the Branch.

The Driver will collect the locked box and key thereto each morning from the Aberystwyth (V. of R.) signal box, and satisfy himself before leaving Aberystwyth that the staff is inside. The driver himself will be responsible for returning the locked box and key to the Signalman on completion of work each evening.

During the period the Branch is worked under "One Engine in Steam" regulations, the tickets for the Branch must be kept in the custody of the Aberystwyth Station Master.

During the time the Aberystwyth (V. of R.) Signal Box is closed the locked box and key thereto must be kept in the Aberystwyth Main Line Signal Box.   (K2)

Page 191

Wrexham (Rhos Jn.) to Rhos and Pant

Delete the following paragraphs :
Legacy—Legacy Level Crossing.
Merseyside and North Wales Electricity Board Sidings.   (K2)

Page 192

Delete the following paragraphs :
Pant Brick Works Siding.
Pant Ground Frame.
Gradients on the Rhos Branch.   (K2)

Page 199

Vale of Rheidol Line—Motor Trolley System of Maintenance

Amend :

Paragraph 2. (One Engine in Steam working) to read :
The Ganger will normally have occupation on the line from Aberystwyth to Devil's Bridge from the time of booking on duty until 2.0 pm daily unless otherwise arranged. The staff for the section will be held by the Aberystwyth Station Inspector during the period of occupation.

Paragraph 1. (Train Staff and Ticket Working) to read :
During the stipulated period, the Single Line is worked by "Train Staff and Ticket" system, the section being Aberystwyth to Devil's Bridge. The instructions on pages 132-134 of the W.R. Regional Appendix will apply for the trolley working in place of Regulation 9 of the Regulations for train signalling on Single Lines by the absolute block system with Train Staff or Train Staff and Ticket working.

Paragraph 2 to read :
The first train from Aberystwyth will be at 10.0 am during this period. The Ganger will normally be allowed occupation of the line from the time of booking on duty at 7.15 am until 9.45 am daily.

Paragraph 3 to read :
The Ganger will contact the Signalman at Aberystwyth at 9.45 am daily or the Devil's Bridge Signalman at 9.55 am and inform him that the line is clear. If contact is made with the Devil's Bridge Signalman, the information must be passed to Aberystwyth (V. of R.) Box.   (K2)

SECTIONAL APPENDIX TO THE WORKING TIME TABLE AND BOOKS OF RULES AND REGULATIONS—NEWPORT TRAFFIC DISTRICT—continued.

★Page 16—Delete Penpergwm and all particulars.
Nantyderry—Amend distance—5 miles 330 yards.   (18.7.64)

Amendments to the Working Instructions dated July 1964.

VALE OF RHEIDOL BRANCH
(Narrow Gauge—1ft. 11½ ins.)

Working Instructions

During the stipulated **Summer period** the Vale of Rheidol Branch Line will be worked by Train Staff and Ticket, such period being announced by special notice.

The Staff and the Tickets will be coloured as follows:
Aberystwyth—Aberffrwd Section—Red
Aberffrwd—Devil's Bridge Section—Blue

The Staff, Tickets and Ticket Boxes for the respective Sections will be kept in the signal boxes and the Signalman will be the only person authorised to receive or deliver a Staff or Ticket. The Staff for the Aberystwyth — Aberffrwd Section will be used for working the Ground Frame at Capel Bangor and the Ground Frames to the Transfer Siding, and Locomotive and Carriage Siding at Aberystwyth.

At the end of each day all cancelled tickets must be forwarded to the Aberystwyth Station Master, who will forward them to the District Traffic Superintendent at the end of each week. At other times the line will be worked under the "One Engine in Steam" regulations.

During the times the line is worked under the "One Engine in Steam" Regulations the staff for each section on the Branch will be kept on the engine in a locked box, the key of which must be kept in possession of the Driver. The staffs in possession of the Driver will be utilised as required to unlock the Ground Frames to gain admission to the various sidings on the Branch.

The Driver will collect the locked box and key thereto each morning from the Aberystwyth (V. of R.) signal box and satisfy himself before leaving Aberystwyth that the correct number of staffs is inside. The Driver will be responsible for returning the locked box and key to the Signalman on completion of work each evening.

During the period the Branch is worked under "One Engine in Steam" Regulations, the Tickets for the respective Sections must be kept in the custody of the Aberystwyth Station Master.

During the time the Aberystwyth (V. of R.) signal Box is closed, the locked box and key thereto must be kept in the Aberystwyth Main Line Signal Box.

The British Railways Arrangements for Working the Railway, dated October 1960.

Coupling and Uncoupling of Vehicles.

No attempt must be made to couple or uncouple Vehicles until they are stationary, and when at rest on a curve the work must be performormed from the outside of the curve.

GENERAL INSTRUCTIONS

Guards must see that wagons are shunted into position immediately on arrival at Aberystwyth. They must also ascertain at starting stations what wagons are to go forward by their respective trains.

Sheets not in use must be carefully folded and returned to Aberystwyth to be stored in the warehouse.

Enginemen must always arrange to have the Engine Tanks filled with water at Devil's Bridge or Aberffrwd on the Down journey.

Guards must carefully examine the loading of Wagons about to be attached to their trains. The weight of the traffic must be evenly distributed on the wagons, and traffic of a bulky nature securely fastened by ropes.

PUBLIC LEVEL CROSSINGS.
Smithfield Road Level Crossing—Aberystwyth.

The normal position of the Level Crossing gates is across the railway and the gates must be constantly closed except when required to be opened for the passage of any trains or engines to or from the station.

The person appointed to open and close the gates and to lower the Signal for either an Up or Down train must be in attendance at the crossing, protecting the roadway by the exhibition of a red handsignal; he will also handsignal each train or engine over the crossing in accordance with Rule 51 Clause (e).

Should it be necessary for trains to pass over this crossing during hours of darkness, an additional member of the Aberystwyth Staff must be provided to instruct the Driver to proceed over the crossing after having first obtained the authority of the person protecting the roadway.

The engine whistle must be sounded when approaching Smithfield Road.

During the night, after the last train has been disposed of, the gates must be secured across the railway by means of a chain and padlock.

Other Public Level Crossings, listed in Table E2, the Driver must sound the engine whistle when approaching the crossing, keep a sharp look out, reduce speed and be prepared to come to a stand before fouling the crossing.

ABERYSTWYTH STATION.

When loaded passenger trains are started from the Dead End, the loop points must be clipped and padlocked for the right direction.

DEVIL'S BRIDGE.
Engines passing each other.

In view of the limited clearance between the Loop Lines, engines must not be allowed to pass each other except at the widest part of the Loop near the Down Starting Signal. When, therefore, it is necessary for a train or engine to be admitted to the station over the Up Loop, whilst an engine is on the Down Loop, the latter must be at a stand at the Down Starting Signal before a train or engine is admitted on to the Up Loop.

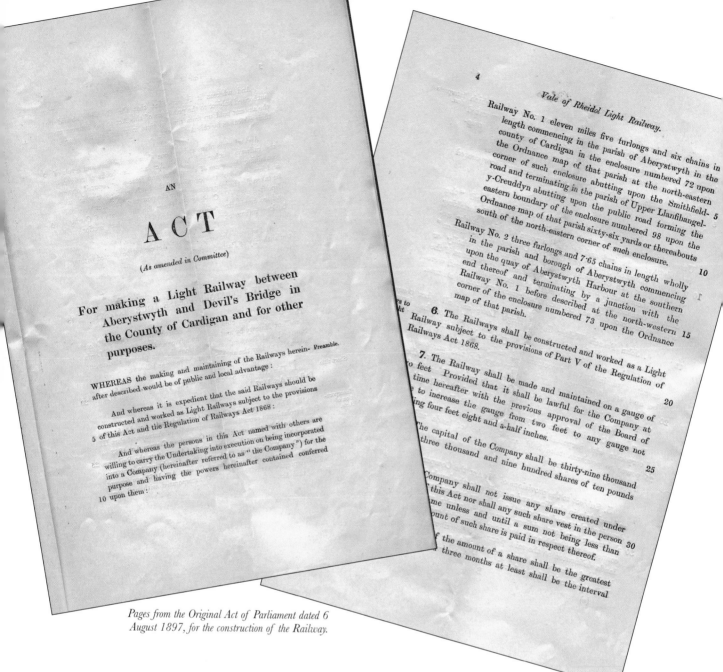

AN

ACT

(As amended in Committee)

For making a Light Railway between Aberystwyth and Devil's Bridge in the County of Cardigan and for other purposes.

WHEREAS the making and maintaining of the Railways herein-after described would be of public and local advantage :

And whereas it is expedient that the said Railways should be constructed and worked as Light Railways subject to the provisions of this Act and the Regulation of Railways Act 1868 :

And whereas the persons in this Act named with others are willing to carry the Undertaking into execution on being incorporated into a Company (hereinafter referred to as " the Company ") for the purpose and having the powers hereinafter contained conferred upon them :

Vale of Rheidol Light Railway.

Railway No. 1 eleven miles five furlongs and six chains in length commencing in the parish of Aberystwyth in the county of Cardigan in the enclosure numbered 72 upon the Ordnance map of that parish at the north-eastern corner of such enclosure abutting upon the Smithfield road and terminating in the parish of Upper Llanfihangel-y-Creuddyn abutting upon the public road forming the eastern boundary of the enclosure numbered 98 upon the Ordnance map of that parish sixty-six yards or thereabouts south of the north-eastern corner of such enclosure.

Railway No. 2 three furlongs and 7·65 chains in length wholly in the parish and borough of Aberystwyth commencing upon the quay of Aberystwyth Harbour at the southern end thereof and terminating by a junction with the Railway No. 1 before described at the north-western corner of the enclosure numbered 73 upon the Ordnance map of that parish.

6. The Railways shall be constructed and worked as a Light Railway subject to the provisions of Part V of the Regulation of Railways Act 1868.

7. The Railway shall be made and maintained on a gauge of two feet Provided that it shall be lawful for the Company at any time hereafter with the previous approval of the Board of Trade to increase the gauge from two feet to any gauge not exceeding four feet eight and a-half inches.

The capital of the Company shall be thirty-nine thousand three hundred shares of ten pounds

Company shall not issue any share created under this Act nor shall any such share vest in the person same unless and until a sum not being less than amount of such share is paid in respect thereof.

of the amount of a share shall be the greatest three months at least shall be the interval

Pages from the Original Act of Parliament dated 6 August 1897, for the construction of the Railway.

Official, Swindon works photograph of locomotive No 8, when new in 1923. The two pipes on the buffer beam are on the right, the vacuum brake pipe, and on the left the steam heating pipe. At the time the new engines were built passenger trains were still run all the year round, and in the winter they were steam heated like their main line brethren.

Aberystwyth's 'Other Railway'

No visit to Aberystwyth should be complete without a trip on its 'Other Railway'! At the extreme north end of the sea front will be found Constitution Hill (430' above sea level), and to help you to get to the top, the longest electrically operated cliff railway in Great Britain will be found. A trip up the hill

View of the cliff railway, with a car on its way up, taken from a car on its way down.

on this railway is well recommended, and when you get to the top, you will find the World's biggest Camera Obscura! What is an Obscura you might ask, well go and have a look!

This railway dates from as long ago as 1896, and is therefore, older than the Vale of Rheidol; it is 778' long, required the remov of no less than 12 000 tons of rock, and wa originally operated on the water balanc principle. By this method the descending ca would have been loaded with water in a larg tank under the passenger seats, and th weight of this would pull the other car up th incline by means of a rop connecting the two cars together an running round a pulley wheel at th top. When the car got to the bottom the water would be emptied ou However, in 1921 this system wa replaced by an electric motor, as wit the water system the water to fill th cars had to be pumped up the hil first! This railway is also unique in s far as cliff railways in this country ar concerned, as the track is undulating whilst all the others are straight.

The railway operates between Easte and October, and from approximately 1000 in the morning unti 1700 in the afternoon - but if you get lef behind by the last car, it is quite easy to wal down! Not only is there the Obscura to be seen on the top of the hill, but excellen views too, and there is a small café fo refreshments.

Another view of Aberystwyth's 'other railway', the cable worked cliff railway that ascends Constitution Hill. Here is a car heading up the incline, with the town and sea front below. April 16 1998.

Bibliography

The Vale of Rheidol Railway, Lewis Cozens; Published by the Author 1950.

The Vale of Rheidol Railway, WJK Davies; Ian Allan - various editions up to 1978.

The Vale of Rheidol Light Railway, CC Green; Wild Swan Publications 1986.

Rheidol Journey, CC Green, Second Edition; Welsh Books Council 1993.